AF328478

MY ARTS!

THE PRIVATE CORRESPONDENCE OF AN ARTS MINISTER

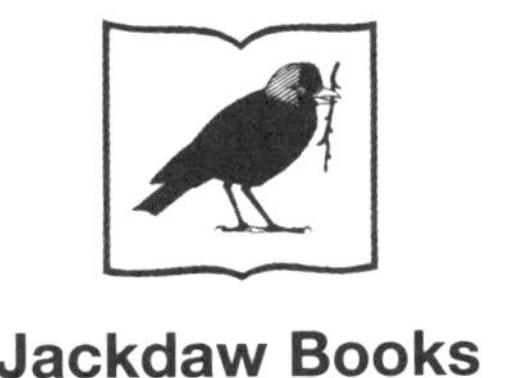

Jackdaw Books

Published by:
Jackdaw Books
Jackdaw Newsletters Ltd
88 Leswin Road London N16 7ND
telephone: 0207-254 4027
mobile: 0777-367 3722
email: dg.lee@virgin.net
www.thejackdaw.co.uk

*

This collection first published 2005. Each report first appeared in
The Jackdaw, a monthly newsletter for the visual arts,
between September 2003 and May 2005.

*

Copyright © Jackdaw Newsletters Ltd
All rights reserved

*

ISBN 0-9550367-0-4

*

Printed and bound in Great Britain

*

Cover drawing by Michael Daley
With thanks to Ian Stephens RE and Nicholas Jolly

Contents

Forward

Dear Tony,

I'd like to present you with the one and only copy of my specially bounded up writings. Actually, this is a bit of a whopper – but let's face it you're no stranger to them yourself eh! – because I had another ten done to give away and keep as mementos of my two years as the country's arts supreemo. I gave one to Geoffrey, my departmental minder, as I was dusting the fluff off my desk. He was sweet and said he'd treasure it and that it had been a truly incredible eye-opener working at my side. He said that as literature it easily ranked alongside Chris Smith's collected speeches and essays as a document that will astonish cultural historians of the future. And there I was thinking that I was never up to the job! It turns out I'm a phenomena! Geoffrey says I'm easily the best woman arts minister since Janet Leigh. Now that I've retired and have the time I might sit down and write a proper book full of difficult words. That is, unless you put me up for the Lords!!! Which I quite fancy!!! I might, just might, even consider a portfoliage!!!

I think that read together in a lump – and it's only a very thin lump after all – my letters make a policy document of real snout for the new millennium and bear full testimony to New Labour's total, full, complete, radical and absolute commitment to an arts policy worthy of the working man of all colours, creeds and capacities. I sincerely believe that during my tennership of this job the working man has been transformed from a fat slob with high blood pressure who farts in his wife's face to a civilised and confident customer of the highest art from Jilly Cooper to Caravedgio. I think you'll agree, Tony, this is no mean achievement.

I'm looking forward to putting my feet up at night from now on and watching some real art on telly with our Con. But don't worry, if your new arts cappo needs any help I'll be only too willing to oblige – the average consultancy rates will do! After all, let's face it Tony, I'm in the knowledge economy now!

Estelle xxxooxxx

P.S. I'd read them in order if I was you.

1

My letter of application
(Doesn't it seem such a long time ago now?)

Dear Tony,

I've heard on the grapevine that you might be considering doing a little Cabinet reshuffle. I decided to write just on the off-chance to tell you that if you happened to be looking for an arts minister then I'd be more than happy to oblige. As you know, and as I've told you before, I'm thicker than a chip butty and, like most of the others who've done the job, I don't really know jack shit about art so I'll be a safe pair of germans perfectly qualified for the job in hand. And I won't have to be fretting all the time like I was with my last job about being made to look daft on that Today programme because with art you can make it all up as you go along and nobody's none the wiser or even gives a toss any road.

I've already set to learning misself that monkey business Chris used to make us all laugh with in the Cabinet. He was a card that Chris! "The arts are an indispensable part of a healthy society". See! That one's word perfect already! "Art is a right not a privillage, a dollop of glue that sticks communities together." There's another! And there's plenty more where they came from believe you me.

Just in case you need me I'm reading that Jilly Cooper book about art so I can hit the ground running.

Always willing to oblige.

TTFN

Department for Culture, Media and Sport
2-4 Cockspur Street
London SW1Y 5DH

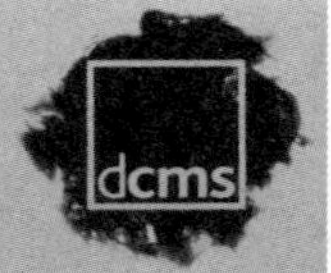

2

My little legs!

Just a few lines Tony to keep you up to spin on what I've been doing in my first month in this lovely new job. You won't regret trusting me with it.

Do you know I haven't stopped. My little legs are worn out. On my very first day no sooner had I opened my lunchbox and crossword book than I was in a limo — with an arm rest in the back seat! — being driven to the Tate Museum. I felt like Marleen Dietrish. Apparently we pay for two of these Tate places in London and another two in the sticks as well, which sounds a bit daft to me, so make no mistake I'll be looking into that wastage at the first opportunity! The one I went to looks like a brick shithouse and has hardly anything in it but escalators and milk bars. I was met at the door by this really weird bloke in a wig and baggy trousers — jesus wept Tony where do we get these creeps from? — who rushed me straight up to room after room full of stripey paintings which made me feel woozy, though I didn't tell him that. This old woman in a cardy, who smelled of smoke and was the spit of my Auntie Agnes from Ardwick Green, took me round and explained to me why she'd painted them and why I was feeling dizzy. It was all some nonsense about landscape vibrations if I understood it proper — honestly though Tony these arty types don't half talk a load of cobblers, just like Chris used to, but at least the bollocks he came out with made us all laugh. Then she took me off to see things

in other rooms that she hadn't painted. You wouldn't
believe some of the shite I saw. In Manchester we get
the bin-men to shift it, but I didn't say so. I was
very diplomatic and only responded with oohs and aahs
like I'd been told to do by my departmental safety net
Geoffrey, who's well into all this crap and was right
up the bloke with the topper. You'd have been proud
of me. I talked the talk, walked the walk and told
them all about Lowry and Henry More.

That first week was all go. On the Wednesday they
hauled me off somewhere called Grimesborne near the
south coast to see an opera. Have you any idea, Tony,
how long an opera is? It's so long they stop for salad
butties in the middle! The story was all my eye and
Peggy Martin too, and what made it worse was they
sang it all in a foreign language. What's the point
of that? I made a mental note to get that one sorted
smartish. Honestly though I was bored to death,
pinching myself all the way through to stay awake.
My poor little thighs are covered in bruises. Every
time my head dropped I had to pretend I was trying
to read the programme. I smiled as often as I could
remember to because I know how keen you are to keep
these arty farties batting for New Labour. But they
don't like us you know! One or two were laughing
behind my back and thought I hadn't noticed but I
had. I get the impression that though they don't like
us they'd rather we were in than the other lot, who
expected them to pay for their own pleasures. Not a
bad idea if you ask me, but mum's the word on that
one eh.

I've done a few announcements too. I'm under
instructions from Geoffrey, who said I'm very good at
announcements, to be very sincere and scholarly so if
you see me on the telly looking really serious you'll
know why. My first appointment was to do with an old
sculpture of a naked woman covering her upstairs and
downstairs, a bit smutty if you ask me. The luvvies
want us to save it from going to America. Eight million
quid! Eight bleeding million! I couldn't believe it.
Phillips Park in Manchester is full of white stone

statues on stands just as good. Me and my best mate Frances Greenhalgh used to tickle their bums with fern stalks and giggle. We had such fun. I think it's been turned into one of them garden centres now.

Anyhow, the worst part of the job by a mile is the constant phone-calls from newspapers trying to trip me up. Last night one reporter shouted "Hey Estelle, who made Michaelangelo's David?" They couldn't catch me out on an easy one like that. "Henry More", I replied, quick as a flash. I remember all about Henry More from when I was teaching in Whalley Range. He was a Lancashire lad like me. And there I am this morning all over the front pages batting for culture. Just leave it me Tony! I'll have those expectations embedded before you can say Jack Robertson!

P.S. I've been dipping into this Irish bloke called James Joyce. Geoffrey suggested I take it on holiday because he said he could tell that Ulissees was right up my alley. Fucking Henry Tony, talk about hard graft. I think there was a few pages missing from my copy so I'm back on Jilly Cooper for homework instead.

3

My office pictures

Honestly though Tony the last four weeks have been hectick. And I mean hectick! You wouldn't believe the decisions I've had to make. The most important was what pictures to hang on my office wall. Apparently, the Government has its own art collection, most of it selected by that creepy article with a topper I was telling you about last month. He does everything that bloke and he's always on the blower moaning about money. He's like that four-by-two in Goodfellas — who sells wigs!!! — who wants his money from the robbery and can't have it and ends up being shot because they get fed up with him asking for it all the time — I'm partial to a good maffia film me. I love that bit in Godfather II where Al Pacino wastes all the other family bosses while he's at the baptism. Brilliant that. Anyway, that patronising twerp with the syrup could do with being taken down a peg or two, or even shot and left in the boot of someone's motor!

God it was hard to choose though. Everything they had in the Government's art collection looked like modern rotten to me. There was nowt by Lowry to start with. Imagine that! Nowt by the most famous artist in Britain! There weren't any nice pictures left so I had to settle for what Geoffrey chose for me. He said I ought to give the impression that I was "catholic in my tastes and attitudes". "But I'm C of E," I said. "I want summat that looks like summat." In the end he insisted I had pictures that made me come across all 'Modern' and 'New Labour' in my thinking as well as being supportive of women artists. So he selected some squiggles by Barbara Hepworth, who as you probably know was Henry More's wife. I could see he was surprised by my knowledge about More. He underestimated me at first but I'm gradually winning him round. I think they look stupid but Geoffrey said you'd be pleased at how I was communicating an open-minded and futurising projection. He's a sweet bloke Geoffrey, such lovely neat shirts for someone who lives on his tod, but I never quite understand what he means. I just hope none of my friends from Manchester notice what I've got on my walls. Believe you me I'll get some crap in the Cheshire Cheese if they see this tripe.

I tell you what though Tony there was a right kerfuffle the other day. I had to make a really important decision about whether to keep a painting by an Italian bloke. 35 million quid! 35 fucking million! I told Geoffrey to stop pulling my knicker elastic. You could buy a fully-equipped hospital in Ancoats for that I told him. Anyway, you know how it is when you can't decide. You can't win. If you say yes you get slagged off and if you say no you get slagged off. In the end I decided to toss a coin and scarper quick after the statement. Then what happens? The night before the announcement that arty-farty know-all from the Evening Standard wrote that it wasn't by who they said it was by and it was really only worth a tenner for the frame. Well, talk about flummoxed. If I'd said yes that bloke on the Today programme would have had me for breakfast. I didn't know what to do so I decided not to make any decision at all, which was brilliant on my part. I put on my haughty teacher's voice, the one I used for the yobs at Whalley Range, and said that I'd require "further consultations" before coming to a final decision. There's no flies on my arse!

And it's been like this all month. Legs worn to stumps. Not stopped. And even after work too. Honestly though Tony, you wouldn't believe the drivel I have to sit through in the evenings when all I want to do is go home, feed the cats, have a spot of tea, stick my cuttings in my album and look in on Eastenders with our Connie. She loves Eastenders does Con. I always get her an Eccles cake on the way home and as soon as that signature tune thumps out she's in there like a ferret up a downspout straight on the settee with her cake scattering crumbs all over the shop. But instead of relaxing in front of something real like that I have to go out and show how "cultivated" I am by sitting through all this tedious crap, plays and that. I thought plays went out with Emergency Ward 10. And by Jesus Tony, there's something else called 'Modern Dance', which Geoffrey loves and keeps roping me in for. It's just an excuse for a strip show! The blokes are all hung like Shergar, balls like granny smiths, and they're all over one another. You don't know where to look. And, guess what, we have to pay for all of it. It's amazing. I can see I'll have to get to grips with them pruning shears. Everywhere you go there's toffs in the audience. There's never any normal folk. And we subsidise the bollocks off all the seats! I mean, get this Tony, we give cheap seats to those who can afford to pay full whack. As our Con said to me the other night "Where's the common in that Ezzie?"

Never mind, keep faith Tony we're getting there.
You can count on me to action and achieve the broadest
widening of outreach and participation.

P.S. By the way, have you ever read Jilly Cooper's
book on art? As you know, it's a bible for me. I
couldn't do without it. She's so knowledgeable. Take
it to Checkers with you, you'll love it.

4

My really important access speech

Bloody Nora Tony, I feel as though I've been on my
little pins non-stop for months. Connie ticked me off
one day last week because I was that busy I didn't
even have time for my favourite Nice 'n' Spicy pot
noodles and Wagon Wheel!

The worst thing this month was that Geoffrey
dropped me right in it again. I had to give a really
big fuck-off speech about "access" and "extending the
remit of participation" when I was opening some festival.
You know, all that core vote arselicking about trying
to get the workers into galleries — we've got to pretend
eh! Any road, I thought it was about time I gave
these arty types a good leathering what for. I was
going to tell them that art galleries aren't just for
nobs with bifocals on the end of their conks but for
us too. I know they're not really for us, because I'm
not interested and most of the working class couldn't give
a bugger either — nobody ever talks about art in the
Cheshire Cheese, it's only ever football, liposuction
and Lanzarotty. Don't worry though I'll pretend that
the workers are interested and that I'm personally
passionately devoted to self-improvement through
museums and the inherent value and regenerational
radicality of the arts — that's another one of
Chris's little phrases by the way. He was a card that
Chris! And what a bugger he was for making up bollocksy
lingo! Any road, I had to play the devil's artichoke
just to pass off we're serious about opening museums
up for the grass roots and the ethnic minorities.

"Why are there never any decent working class folk in art galleries?" I was going to ask giving them my stern, over-the-spectacles daggers look. And the answer, which I was going to give myself because it wasn't really a question for them to answer because I was really going to answer it myself all along, was that the people who run museums, like that bloke with the topper and baggy pants who's always on the blower for more lolly, are all university toffs who hate the workers and pretend that art's really hard and requires everyone to think it's good whatever they think of it. And it's true the poor old workers can't follow the stories or see what's what. And it's not the ethnic minorities' fault they'd rather spend their time getting fatter and fatter and buying jewellery and loading up their Toyotas with Mr Pataks at the cash and carry.

I was going to straighten out these snooty wankers and tell them that until they put tellies and armchairs in the corner of each gallery they're not getting any more ackers. That'd have showed em. Then what happens but Geoffrey leaks what I'm going to say to that know-all from the Evening Standard, him who stitched me up last time over that Italian picture that's only worth coppers. He said I'm an ignorant know-nowt who wouldn't know one end of a Bottycello from the other. I told him good and proper that I know all about Henry More and the Victoria and Arthur because I had the kids do projects on them. All because of him the whole world was suddenly against me, accusing me of dummindown, whatever that is, so I had to re-jig and in the end I told them that they were doing a good job, but only if they put big boards on the wall saying what everything's about. I've had the last laugh though because they think they're getting more money, and they're damn well not!!! As our Connie always says: "You weren't called Iron Knickers for nothing Ezzie."

Jesus wept Tony — and believe me, Jesus would have bloody well wept at this — I had to sit through something called The Ring Circuit at Convent Garden the other day. Geoffrey said he thought I'd be challenged by the plot's political intrigues and symbolism, but it was in French and I'm not joking it lasted longer than the Embassy snooker final. Ronnie O'Sullivan could have knocked up three or four maximum breaks before they even started singing — between you and me our Connie wouldn't mind giving Ronnie O's cue a good chalking! The only good bit was in the middle when they played the theme tune from 633 Squadron. Do you know it took all day and it was only half over even then. I bunked off the second day claiming a much-regretted sudden emergency in my constituency. There's no flies on my arse!

The National Gallery, which as you might know is in London, asked me to choose a painting this month and say what I thought about it; you know, to make it look as though ordinary folk like me can have a worthwhile opinion about art. Shrewd as ever I chose one by Turner which is old but modern too. It's called Iron, Rain and Fog. It looked a bit blurry to me in the postcard but Geoffrey explained that Turner was known for atmosphere not detail. It strikes me as barmy if you can't see what it's supposed to be so I wrote that coming from Manchester I identified with the rain and the fog. In fact it reminded me of trains going across Stockport viaduct in the old days of smoking mills and pea-soopers and my dad setting off for the works in winter. You know, all that brass band and Hovis bollocks.

That's all for now. You'll be pleased to know I'm well on the way to delivering the luvvy vote.

5

My encounter with the fairies

Blood and sand Tony, don't tell anyone for Christ's sake but you wouldn't believe the number of fairies in the art world. It's crawling with em. Everywhere you look there's blokes in leather pants smoking with their fingers out like that posh sailor in the war films. Connie was telling me I'd have to watch out for them because you know how unpredictable they can be. One minute you're best pals and swapping phone numbers and the next you've rubbed them up the wrong way and they're clawing the clothes off your back and stamping their loafers like redskins on the warpath. Of course, because I'm politically correct like all of us in the New Labour project I don't let on that I think they're any different to the rest of us. I've become convinced that everyone's queer in the theatre, and you'd never guess with some of them. People you thought were as normal as you and me turn out to be screamers when you meet them behind the scenes, mincing about, calling each other bitches and pinching one another's behinds. Geoffrey was telling me that one of our knighted actors — no names mentioned but — is shacked up with a bloke who drives a truck for Eddie Stobart! I tell you, they wouldn't get past the door in the Cheshire Cheese but they flounce into my office pouting and tapping on the desk, throwing their arms about demanding to know what we're going to do about gay theatre and lesbian film collectives and saying it's about time they had their own department in the Arts Council so that they can spend their own conkers on whatever tickles their fancies... And you can't tell them anything. As soon as you try they're off ranting again. Chris must have felt well at home. Geoffrey keeps telling me that he'll handle the nancy boy and dungaree end of things. They're prepared to listen to him whereas I can't get a word in edgewards, they just sit there ignoring what I say squirting smoke at the No Smoking sign.

I had to trek miles up the east coast last week to unveil a sculpture dedicated to some famous composer. I missed The Bill because the traffic coming back on the M11 was so bad. This sculpture thing cost a quarter of a million and looked like a scrapheap. Luckily, they thought I loved it but my expression was disbelief not enthusiasm. Jesus Tony, there's a fitter from British Aerospace, an ordinary bloke with a cleff palette from Chorlton-on-Medlock who comes in the Cheshire Cheese. In his spare time he welds scrap metal into fantastic animals and machines and he could've done something really smashing for a couple of hundred. Anyway, Geoffrey wrote me a speech about "challenging innovative forms" and "new progressive ways of looking" and "raising the quality of life for the working man" and the need to be open-minded about original and unfamiliar work which we weren't used to looking at yet — all the usual cobblers. I faked sincerity when I read it out but really the sculpture was horrible. I felt embarrassed to have my photograph taken in front of it and I felt sorry for the poor bastards who lived right next door. Connie would never speak to me again if I unveiled such an Isaw at the end of our path.

Hey, you'll never guess what Tony, I was asked to open some new galleries in the Victoria and Arnold which, as I've told you, I know a lot about. Of course you can't drive past it now because they've pedestrianised Trafalgar Square. It's a great honour to be asked apparently. The Queen usually does it but she had the leopard-skin leotard brigade at Balmoral that week — she'll have had to padlock the spoons for those kleptos eh? Any road, somebody wrote me a really heavyweight policy speech about the importance of art as an energising ingredient in a full and wholesome life — you know, all that drivel Chris used to make us laugh with. It got us lots of good coverage in the papers without costing us a brass farthing! And of course the best thing is it was all waffle and didn't commit us to anything at all. I called my speech 'Who put the Art in Scunthorpe?', Scunthorpe being a marginal! Clever stuff eh! There's no flies on my arse!

God, this job can be boring though sometimes. Everywhere I go there's a line-up waiting to shake my hand and no sooner have I finished than one of them's pestering me for more brass. I nearly lost it last week. One bloke kept asking and asking while he was showing me round an exhibition of complete junk

— which we'd paid for of course! — by someone who'd won the Turner Award. I felt like kicking him because I've heard it all before til I'm blue in the face. Geoffrey, on the other hand, is good at letting them down slowly. He listens very attentively, nods his head like a vicar, makes encouraging grunts, and takes armfuls of hand-outs and glossy brochures which are, naturally, lobbed straight into the shredder as soon as we get back to the office.

By the way, I hope you enjoyed Jilly Cooper's book on art while you were in Egypt. Isn't it a bible just? I sent it to all my friends for Christmas. I'm thinking of recommending her as the next supreemo of the Arts Council. What do you think?

6

My orsum dilemma with dishonesty

Tony, you're going to be proud of me. I've been walking my little legs to stumps doing openings here, speeches there and clapping till my hands are chapped. But do you know, this job's one disadvantage is that I've to keep pretending all the time. Everything I see I've to pretend I like even though most of it's pointless to my way of looking. I'm never allowed to say what I think. I don't want to come over feelysophical, but you just wonder when you talk to someone in the arts if they really believe what they say they believe, or are they just saying it because they think they ought to say it, while really they know that you know that's what they're doing. Have I lost you? I sometimes think it's all just a game where nobody tells the truth. So much of what I see means nothing to me. Take this week: I went to a film opening about a painter called John something, Dutch he was, because we all had to troop out to give support for the British film industry in spite of the fact that most of the films my department pays for are such a load of crap they never get released. As Connie said: "Where's the sense in that Ezzie? Why don't you tell them to piss off and make films people want to watch." Well Tony, you've heard about watching paint dry, well this was like fucking listening to it dry as well! Bloody Nora, there was no special effects nor nowt and the characters never said anything but just scowled at each other and then stood looking out of the window for ages. The actors must have knocked up ten grand a word each. Needless to say for what it cost we could have fed and watered most of Africa for a year or more. The audience was raving over it. Geoffrey said it was about the dawning of light and love and beauty in a young girl's sikey, whatever that is. It goes without saying, I told them I loved it.

Then the next night I had to do a lot of pretending at a gallery in the East End where the Turner Award is fixed. All there was was bags of rubbish around the place. The artist told me, all intellectual like, as though he was explaining black holes to a turnip, that what he was doing was a kind of visual joke because most people think contemporary art is a load of rubbish — not half eh? — and this is a load of rubbish which is actually rather a good load of rubbish. He lost me. Geoffrey said it was challengingly ironic and he was, as usual, right up that self-important twat with the topper who's always on the blower for more dosh. Come to think of it, wiggins was at the film too. In fact, nearly everyone who'd been at the film the night before was here too. I thought I was going to meet lots of different folk when I took on this job but I meet all the same people every week and they all dress up like Danny Laroo. Nobody wears proper clothes. Anybody would think we've only got three artists. And when they're not all meeting one another at dos they're all at award ceremonies giving one another prizes. Seems a bit incestious to me. If they don't have people making it for them it makes me wonder when they actually get their work done.

Anyway, I whispered to Geoffrey that I thought the work was a load of rubbish. And he said that's exactly what you're supposed to say. But I really do think

it's a load of rubbish, I said. He patted me and
whispered, all knowingly like, that the Topper had
explained to him that it was obviously a submersive
take on mortality, you know death and that, and that
one way or another we all end up in the plastic binliner
of history. These folk'll believe anything. Then he
told me that the Topper wanted to buy this junk for
his museum and would I like to contribute a few grand
of spondoolies. I nearly dropped my Ritz cracker when
he told me how much. I tell you what Tony, it's a rum
world when a bag of rubbish costs more than a row of
homes in Stretford. Of course, I told them it was
very intellectually stimulising and stopped on the
way home for some chips.

You're never going to believe this one Tony. I had
to go to a concert one night because a very important
American composer was over punting for work. Jesus,
call me a Phyllis Stein but what a load of earache
it was. They were all over him too, and do you know
what his most famous work was? Nothing. There was no
notes in it nor nowt. Before it started Geoffrey
leaned over and told me to listen very carefully to
the next piece "because it deals with silence". We
sat there for ages and nothing started up, and that
was it! We nearly got in trouble though. I'd taken
Connie along for a treat and after a while of wondering
what was happening she said in a loud voice "I think the
conductor's had a seizure Ezz". Them in front turned
round and told her to shut up and listen. At the end
of it there was loud applause and people standing up
cheering. And afterwards the American said it had
been one of the most moving performances he could
remember. I kept expecting the bloke from Candid
Camera to pop out from behind the curtains. I can't
work out if it's them or me that's gone completely
bonkers. I told the composer he was very clever to
pull that one off, and I bloody well meant it too.
You've got to hand it to a bloke who can make people
believe they've heard something when not a note's
been blown.

Must dash, I'm well late for I'm a Celebrity!

7

My friend Pickles

Tony, don't get me wrong, I don't want to come across all, y'know, feelysophical again but when I think about it too much I get hopelessly confused about this job. Sometimes I think I just sign cheques — which those who receive them always say is never enough — open exhibitions, sit in the pound seats fast asleep on first nights, make speeches saying the same things over and over, read out statistics that Geoffrey's made up to make it seem that art's more popular than ever before, meet people who want more money or tell me what to do ... while all around me everything goes on as it always did. I sometimes think we don't really need an arts minister. Life wouldn't stop would it? Let's face it Lowry would have painted Daisy Nook whether or not I was sat in my office. And Dickens didn't need the Arts Council to write Withering Heights did he? It's not as though I can affect anything and, as I told you last time, I'm not allowed to tell the truth any road.

Pickles, a mate of mine in the Cheshire Cheese, brought it all home to me last weekend. While Connie was on the karaoke he sidled over to the fruit machine and said he'd seen me on the telly opening that new exhibition at the Tate, the one with a six-legged calf trapped inside some double glazing. Believe me Tony, Pickles is a decent working bloke, a joiner and fitter, who's in our quiz team because he knows about sport, the history and everything. We call him 'Pickles' because he's very proud of his shallots — he has an allotment on the ring road up Sharston way. If we were talking, you and me, off the record, we'd probably agree that Pickles is a bit unsophisticated — he's never lived down London like us. Like me, he doesn't understand about art but he wants to, and he doesn't understand when something

23

can't be explained in a way so he understands it, like art for example.

I find myself having to justify to Pickles a lot of what goes on in my department while wishing I didn't have to because even though he's uneducated he often has a clever point to make. Just because he hasn't read Jilly Cooper, like I have, and doesn't know about Henry More, like what I do, it doesn't mean he's always wrong. Any road, he told me that what I was looking at was in his view, and in the opinion of his mates on the site, "a complete and utter load of shite". He said it looked like a fairground and that if he went to an art gallery he'd want something more than badly made bad jokes about monkeys playing with themselves — if he wants to see that he can go to Chester Zoo. I told him that I agreed with him and that it was so childish it made me laugh. And I can tell you Tony, it made me laugh even more when the bloke with the topper who's always on the blower for more dosh told me what they were supposed to be about. You'd never have guessed. I couldn't take it seriously. Pickles asked me why I didn't do something about it. Wasn't I supposed to be the boss? Yes I am, I said, but they're the experts and they know and we don't. He said, what is it they know that makes them able to say that a truckdriver playing with himself in his cab is better and more important art than the animals Bryan — one of our mates in the Cheshire Cheese — welds from scrap in his back yard? I've told you about Bryan before, he's a machine operator for Ciba-Geigy and very gifted with his hands. He's knocked up a brilliant ostrich from beer tins which Pickles has for safe keeping in his lock up.

I thought the bloke playing with himself was pathetic too, but I told Pickles it was about how women are demeaned and threatened and made to feel like sex objects. He said he knew all that already. In fact he'd heard the same story a million times over and why did he have to be told in the most disgusting way something everybody already knows. I told him again that they know better than us because they're looking at it every day. Then he asked me why I was so frightened of them, so scared to say what I thought. He said we might not be Henry Kissinger but we're not stupid so why can't they explain to us why it's so good when it looks so poorile. He said he wanted to see what they saw but could only see what he saw himself and it was nothing like what they were seeing. I told him to get away because he'd obviously had too many. And anyway, I said, putting on my teacher's voice, I'm not frightened of them so there. At that moment Connie came over, put her arm on Pickles' shoulder and told him that there was no point in talking common sense to me because nobody in the arts ever understands a word of common.

I tell you what though Tony, our Con's right. And Pickles is right anall, I am frightened of them. These people are as single-minded as terrorists. They won't admit the possibility they're wrong and they've got a way of looking at you as though you're blind and dead thick with it. I told Geoffrey what Pickles had said and he told me to ignore the likes of him because his sort would never understand that some people can see better than others.

Must dash. TTFN

8

My brush with a proper painting

Strictly between us Tony it's all QT and Bristol shape on the culture front. Fingers crossed, it's working smoother than a shithouse door in Bombay, as our Connie says. We've been working away behind the lines smarming the luvvys in the run-up to the next election. We'll be able to point to targets met and concrete, actual, verifiable, literal and radical changes all leading to an upgrade in the quality of life. And Geoffrey said he's even thought of a clever way to fiddle the figures to make it look as though nearly everyone who visits the British Museum is black. I've got him thinking straight at last.

Just look at our accomplishments: we've saved that Maradona and Child for the National Gallery which is by a very important artist; all the museums have got smashing caffs and gift shops and it doesn't look as though any will rock the boat by charging or going bust in the near future; the theatres have had a lick of paint and actors are earning a few bob above the minimum wage; we've got the LSE touring their 'Rockin All Over The World' orchestrial pop greats; the Royal Bally are doing a brake dance version of Porky and Bess at the Hackney Empire; and the Royal Shakespeare Corporation are up north with 'The Merry Footballers Wives of Windsor' ... I think you'll agree it's a transformation from the stuck up Toff Art we inherited. I hauled in that big woman we've just put in to run the Arts Council and told him in my I'm-in-charge voice that he can spend all he wants on his pet projects, including hisself (he thinks I don't know he trousers a few quid for his school you know!), but he's got to guarantee that next year there's no white elephants going bollocks up before they open because his 'experts' are so fuckin useless they couldn't catch aids in Uganda. I also told him there's to be none of those subsidised pillocks traipsing over Mow Cop dressed as Mongolian Diddymen neither.

All in all I've had time to be seen about enjoying the fruits of New Labour's labours, as you might say. I'm visiting museums incogneeto at lunchtime to keep tabs. Luckily the National Gallery's just across the back entry from my office. They've got stuff in there Tony that's hundreds of years old but shiny as a new tanner, as though it was painted last week! And it's crowded so you can't see owt or get any peace and quiet. They haven't got anything by Lowry or Henry More but I've been looking at Turner, a landscape painter who lived a while back in the Industrial Rebellion.

I'm beginning to get the hang of this art caper. There's more to it than meets the eye. I was looking hard at that picture Turner did of a train the other day, the one I had to write about a while back but which I hadn't actually seen in the buff. At first I couldn't see much but once my eye was in I got lost in it. It was like watching a good serial on telly. The engine was black as though it was painted with soot. It was spitting fire from red-hot glowing coals in the boiler. He made it like a wild dog rushing across a bridge over a river, a bit like the one Lowry used to paint in Stockport, but not as good. It was suddenly frightening. It was as though a fiery beast had been uncaged from Belle Vue and was coming out of nowhere straight at you down Hyde Road. The rest of the picture is unclear, like the view from a train window when it's pouring down. I was just about to move along when I noticed that there's a rabbit on the tracks right in front of the train running like mad trying to escape but it can't. The picture suddenly moved up a speed and the train became an unstoppable hunter raging out of a storm trying to kill a frightened animal. I started dwelling on what the cruel monster of new industry could do to the world if we didn't have a thoughtful engine driver with his hands firmly on the brake and the warning whistle. Tony, I was so taken aback and shaken by what was in this painting I had to rest my little legs. For the first time I realised what all these fairies I deal with are on about. I told Connie when I got home but couldn't drag her away from Holby City. She told me to button it and said I probably needed more of my hot flush tablets.

The next day I was on my way to the British Museum when someone stopped me in Trafalgar Square. "What do you think of this Estelle?", blurted some loudmouth pointing at two lads sat in a glass kiosk. "It's art." he said. "Course it isn't," I told him. "Stop trying to catch me out. It's two blokes flogging bird seed." "It's art", he said, and came out with some rot about the passage of time, like that bloke with a topper who's always on the blower for more lolly. I said if it's art the person who's paying for it's a bloody fool. "You're paying for it", he said. I laughed. As though we'd would waste hard-earned lolly on cobblers like that. "It's funded by the Arts Council," he said. "Stop being daft," I shouted dead indignified and told him to go and look at some proper stuff in the National Gallery, which of course won't cost him a bean thanks to us making it free. I can see I'm going to have to have another stern word with that swaggering jessie at the Arts Council.

9

My dinner hour in the British Museum

Tony, I've been thinking. You know I've been trying to get New Labour's traditional historical constituency to go to art galleries instead of watching Emmerdale and eating and supping all the time and putting a strain on the health service? Well, I told Connie the other day that instead of sitting there all night waiting for Charlie Dimmock to bend over and stuffing down Thornton's nutty slack she'd be better off studying Rembrandt's etchings. She said, "With his dress sense Rembrandt could do with a good makeover. Give me that Jack Vettriano any day. I'd go up any time to twang his braces let alone scratch his itchy etchings." She can be a bit of a card our Con can. And do you know Tony, I think she would. And she's got a point. What's so wrong with popular art when it's what so many folk want to see? But if you say this to that Hitler with the topper he treats you as though you've just been let out for the afternoon!

Whenever I think about the grass roots, those people who vote for us because we're not posh, I always have Pickles in mind. He's typical of our supporters is Pickles. He works hard, earns a decent wage, pops in the Cheshire Cheese three or four times a week for a few pints of Boddies and a Thai nosebag, has a fortnight every summer at his sister's in Workington and goes to his allotment for a contented smoke of a weekend. He does lovely shallots — his nickname you see! — but I don't know what else he grows. Any road, we're barking up the wrong tree Tony. Pickles is never going to be interested in art galleries or museums. He just isn't. And neither's Connie. Their lives are full already. Pickles doesn't need art or culture any more than he needs long words to express hisself. Unfortunately for all those who promote art as "an empowering force for improvement", as Chris used to say, no Saturday morning will ever dawn when Pickles and his like wake up, stare at the dry rot on the ceiling and think: "I know, I'll make misself a nice brew then get the 109 into town to see the Turner seascapes at the art gallery. Then praps I'll treat misself to a foreign stew and a frapperchino in the caff while I'm at it." It's not going to happen Tony! And I can't make it happen! So there's no point in pretending that I can. And it's no use Gordon telling me off neither for not achieving the impossible in the name of social justice and equality of opportunity. We can't change the way people are and it's wrong of us to think we can. Of course, Geoffrey says we shouldn't try: "Art's too good for these people. Your better off leaving them to their prize-winning onions and pork pie hats." Between you and me I can't stand Geoffrey sometimes, he doesn't know any more what's going on than you or me. He's like everybody else round here, he's so terrified of the truth he tells whoppers all the time and thinks he's dead clever for doing it — a bit like you Tony, but mum's the word.

As I told you last month, I've been stepping out at dinner time to keep tabs on them who moan about not having enough cash. You wouldn't believe the British Museum Tony. You should go. You breeze straight in, no queues for cash registers, lovely signs everywhere and helpful attendants dozing in the corners, and within seconds of dodging buses you're looking at a Greek temple as though you was stood next to it in Corfu. Mind you, I had no idea Elgin's marbles were in such a state, but do you know Tony they touched me. It was as though the damage added to the sadness. There's this headless woman with no brazier wearing a long nightie over her big motherly legs, just like my mum's. For a minute I thought I was looking at Henry More. As you know I'm well up on Henry because I got the kids to do projects on him. But don't you think it's wonderful how two artists hundreds of centuries apart could be inspired just by a woman sat ready for bed warming her husband's tea by the fire. I sometimes wish I could get Pickles to make time to come with me so he could just stand and look. He'd be as surprised as I've been. And do you know the place is packed with Japs. They never seem to stop laughing and they're a damn nuisance shuffling about the place like clouds of midges. They never look at anything proper and just line up to have their photos taken beside the bare women. Come to think of it we ought to think of a way of charging all these foreigners to see our best stuff. I'll get Geoffrey working on that one.

By the way, tomorrow I'm off to Can, which is near Paris in France, to see some of their films while talking up ours. The department knocked me up a video of the bits I've to see so I can prepare my usual canny — !!! — observations about this noovle varg caper Geoffrey's always going on about. I watched them with Connie last Saturday before Casualty. They were nothing like Whistle Down The Wind, which is my favourite favourite film of all time, and terribly hard to follow because they had what was being said written across the bottom in English. Con stormed off to the Cheese. She said "What's the point of making films in Polish when only the fucking Poles can understand them?" I had to admit it's going to be hard graft sitting through that lot, but at least it'll be nice and sunny and Geoffrey promised me I might get to meet Hayley Mills so I'll keep my autograph book at the ready.

10

My trip to Can

Oh Tony Tony Tony, by the ten men and a lad you wouldn't believe Can! What a job this is! Talk about rat-arsed every night! I still can't believe I'm paid to go to the pictures all day, even if most of them are arty piffle. The trouble with these difficult films is they go on and on and hardly anything happens. No wonder they can't get funding for them, except from me of course. And if you've had a few free schooners and a pile of curry sandwiches before you go in you're snoring the rafters off before the actors' names have stopped. I just wanted to be out in the sunshine really, but I passed off I was interested and told everyone of our absolute, total and complete commitment to a vigorous, challenging and inclusive British film industry. I'm positive they all swallowed it.

I'll start at the beginning, which, as they sing in one of my all-time favourite films, is a very good place to start! We flew into a place called Nice, which is pronounced neece but which was very nice! Lovely blue sea, palm trees, pancake stands and sailing yachts, just like Lytham on Whit Monday except for the palm trees and pancake stands. Can's a bit further up the coast. Nobody told me it was on the sea else I'd have brought a cozzy. There's a long prom called the Croissant where all the famous people walk at night showing off their tans and flashing their new togs from Next and naturally there's a terrible lot of cinemas and waiters. The really swanky folk stay on their own boats which are lined up like Salford Marina. We stayed in a hotel right on the Croissant which was lovely Tony, stuffed with goodies to take home. The bathroom had dozens of little bottles which I salted away every day so they'd put more in and there was even a little sewing set and some novelty balloons in different flavours which I've saved — a nice present for the nieces from Nice!!

Then what happens but the very first night I meet Rudolf Valentino! He looked amazingly young though he's losing his hair. He was one of the judges and told me a thing or two about British cinema. He asked me if I'd seen his film Reservation Dogs, a cowboy I think, but I told him that I don't get much time off as a minister and that naturally I knew all his old films where he was wearing lots of sexy mascara and cavorting in and out of tents and that. Then that interfering poofter Geoffrey took him away just as I was about to ask for his autograph for my auntie Ethel. The film we saw was Turkish I think. There were a lot of goats with bells on and twangy music but then I went spark out. "It'll be the jet lag," Geoffrey said. It bloody well won't! I was pissed as a monkey!

The first morning was beautiful. With the sun blazing in through the French windows I had my breakfast on a tray in bed watching Sky. Just like being at home, except here they have crusty bread and jam and coffee in a soup bowl instead of Cheerios and Quick Brew.

Just between you and me Tony, I came expecting to fiddle a good few bob on my expences but I didn't get the chance. Everywhere we went there was lashings of free grub and booze and you could go back as many times as you wanted. With three films a day and spreads at every one I was full to spewing by bedtime. Connie, who arrived the second day on Ryanair, was a bit picky at first with it being foreign but once she got her eye in she was well paralytic and stuffing her handbag full of keesh wrapped in serviettes. This place is paradise. Everywhere you go there's women with virtually nowt on and blokes with dyed hair who can't stop laughing. Sadly, I didn't spot Hayley Mills all week.

Everyone was talking about Roger Moore, who's put on an awful lot of weight and looks like he's a bit down on his luck. He's made a film about 9/11 which says that international terrorism was all George Bush's fault for being related to a shake in Saudi Arabia. There was no story to it but guess what Tony, you were in it a couple of times! Anyway, Roger, who was a bit too full of himself I thought and refused to talk to me because I was a friend of yours, ended up winning something called the Palm Door, which Geoffrey tells me is a gold miniature of the door of the very first cinema, the Palm naturally, in Soho. It beats me how he knows all this stuff.

I was well sad to leave Can because it was like being a carefree child again on holiday, but no sooner was I back than I was off for a book festival in Hay-on-Why. I was asked to talk about my taste in literature. Geoffrey briefed me on the things he thought I ought to say I liked and kept permanently on my bedside table, next to Jilly Cooper of course. He also gave me a summary of each book in case the wise guys from the press tried to trip me up. I was a bit worried I'd get confused with which characters were in which books but I ended up being very entertaining and everybody said it was the funniest evening of the week. One of the organisers even said that he was going to make a special effort to read Great Exploitations on the strength of my recommendation. Believe me Tony we've got the luvvy vote by the short and curlies!

11

My unexpected meeting with Chris!

Well Tony it's been back to normal this month after all the gallivanting abroad, what with Can and Wales. And I forgot about the Baltic too! I was surprised to find that the Baltic is quite like parts of England and that they all speak passable English there, though of course it's tricky getting the gist at first. It was also reassuring to know that they seem to have the same funding problems in Scandinavia, which as you might already know is where Balticland is. You'll never guess what though Tony, the arts complex I visited is run by an Irish bloke from Stockport who knows the Cheshire Cheese! We had a proper good matey laugh about that. I told him that what with him commuting every week to these foreign climes he was a living example of how the global village is affecting even art. I asked him if he was bothering to learn the language but he said he seemed to be coping alright so far.

After I'd flown back from the Baltic I had to do the honours at a new centre, one of the only ones I've opened which, one way or the other, we haven't had to cough up for. It's a kind of management hothouse for artyfarties to make sure that in the future we have people of sufficient calibber to run our best arts organisations. It'll train them up to mix suavely with the super wealthy and learn them to add up as well as talk and write that tripe they all come out with. Apparently we haven't got anyone coming up the ladder who can take over from him with that daft topper who keeps coming on the blower because he's short for his rent. I'm told there are very few with the necessary skill to ask persuasively for more cash, especially from filthy rich blokes who need their arms twisting a bit with honorary degrees and the promise of knighthoods before they'll sign on the dotted spondooly. I used it as an opportunity to tell them in no uncertain terms that in the future if they want more money it's absolutely essential to have the most talented, knowledgeable and well-trained folk batting for art and doing the necessary begging, otherwise they'll all be on the breadline and make no mistake. Believe me Tony, one day we'll get value for money out of all these self-righteous nancy boys.

Any road, I rolls up to cut the ribbon of this supposed seedbed of new talent and who should open the car door but my predecessor Chris! He's a right one to be running an organisation for good organisers — it was him who did that millennium marquee that got us in so much lumber. I know he's a lovely bloke but he couldn't sell diarrhoea pills in Delhi. Connie nearly thrutched herself laughing when she heard he was in charge. I found one of his speeches in a bottom drawer the other day. It was one of them he used to read us in that funny voice when he was on about "the arts being at the very nucleus of our radical cultural mission". Chris! Training the most talented leaders of the future! I mean, Tony, talk about a joke.

Now then, to more serious matters. I was in the Cheshire Cheese a good while back fullfilling some urgent constituency business when a bloke came up and said he was from the Whitworth. I thought he was probably the manager of a pub up Whitworth Park but it turns out that Manchester University has an art gallery down Moss Side way which is open to the public but which is broke because they can't reclaim their VAT like other museums. He was very pushy and wouldn't take no for an answer so instead of watching Jensen Button on the telly I had to waste Sunday afternoon traipsing up to this place. I knew the building of course but I'd always thought it was the clap clinic or something else belonging to the Royal Infirmary opposite. While I was having my ear bent Connie came up and whispered all astonished like, "You'll never believe it Ezz but it looks as though they've got some proper stuff here, pictures and that." And so it was Tony. There's a room full of Lowrys to start with and you can't beat that! One of them was of the streets off Oldham Road where my dad was born. This is more like it, I thought. And apparently there's lots of places like this one all round the country. Since then I've been working tirelessly behind the scenes trying to get Gordon to allow universities to reclaim their VAT so that these places can remain open free and have a bit put by for publicity, dos and whatever. Anyway he's finally come up trumps, testimony to my successful lobbying skills and persuasive arguments, as Geoffrey assured me. This might not seem like much to you Tony but I'm savvier than I sound. You can shut these arty types up for coppers. Call it buying votes if you like but let's face it we've all got our jobs to protect and there's no way I'm going back to teaching those savages in the comprehensives. So leave the luvvy vote to me pal!!!

12

My summer holiday

There's no rest for me Tony! Even on holiday here I am on the shayslong reading Jilly Cooper again so I can get back to the grindstone even more clued up than when I left. What that woman doesn't know about art isn't worth a fig and it's so clever the way she manages to make you feel as though you're enjoying yourself while learning something about proper culture. For example, in her book about art there's quite a lot of how's-your-father if you get my meaning, but in between there's fascinating information about Raffles who was a famous artist especially renowned, it turns out, for liking a bit of how's-your-father himself.

For our holidays this year Connie and I went for Turkey. We tried Italy last year but found there wasn't enough to see and the food was muck. It's better here, scorching hot, cheaper than a Newton Heath tart, the grub's the same as in Manchester and — you'll never believe this Tony — it's full of very old ruins. They're everywhere but not a one Turkish. They're all Greek and Roman! In Turkey! Connie hasn't bothered herself much with the sites because, between you and me, she's hitting the Montezuma pills and anyway she said if she wants to see ruins she can go round Longsight and Moss Side when she gets home. I've been to a place called Efissus but I didn't let on who I was in case the Turks thought I was spying for the British Museum. Geoffrey told me to keep stum and said that he knew I'd want to spend at least a whole day following in the footsteps of St Paul. Believe you me Tony it's wall-to-wall rubble at Efissus and thousands of red-faced folk tramping about kicking up dust and gagging for a cold drink wishing they were in the sea. I couldn't make head nor tail of it. There was a lovely view of the coast though from the theatre which was really just a lot of steps in a semi-circle, a bit like the Gaumont on Oxford Road but without the roof. It was a sun trap and not a sign of a dressing room. I couldn't have watched Tommy Cooper in that heat never mind a lot of naked blokes wearing funny masks and talking dirty. The audience in those days must have boiled alive and the stone terraces must have been murder for anyone whose chalfonts were bubbling — that's another good job Connie didn't come! What this place needed was some of the stuff in the British Museum to liven it up, a few statues or bits of animals and proper architecture with doors and windows. And as for the Wonder of the World, a temple down the road, it was a single column with a stork's nest on the top surrounded by gyppoes charging top whack for slivers of water melon and tea towels with Brad Pitt on playing Ivanhoe. It beats me what anybody could possibly see in it. I was glad to get back to the beach.

Anyway, as the arts have been a bit quiet since we last spoke I wanted to recap on the year and reassure you that the luvvy vote is boxed and gift-wrapped. On the plus side we've sold everyone the idea that museums are free to get in and that if there's any problems it's down to museum incompetence and definitely not our fault. All the grants have gone up at more than the rate of inflation — at least that's the spin! The museums are packed out, mainly with foreigners but don't tell anyone. We've bought stacks of pictures which were threatened with going abroad. There's more ethnic minorities and grass-root types going to theatres and opera than ever before — we can run up some numbers or invent a survey to prove that if we have to. And we've got the pansy administrators thinking popular for once. The downside is that whatever we do they're all forever moaning about being broke and the Arts Council are always making us look daft by spending serious money on stuff any dozy bugger could see is a waste of space. The week before I came away I had to go and open an upside-down tree in the grounds of a Bristol hospital. Honestly though Tony, where's the art in that? It's all very well Geoffrey telling me to be open minded but as Pickles in the Cheshire Cheese said to me after he'd seen it on the telly: "What they going to do when it has to just stand there and speak for itself." He's got a point. That laughing boy with the topper was giving out about "investigating nuances of life and death" but when someone who doesn't know what it is rolls up tomorrow morning after the fuss has died down will they even see it as art? And if they don't why are those pillocks at the Arts Council shelling out thirty grand of our money on it? Of course, I told them that, cutting edgely speaking, I thought it was very challenging, subversant and definitely a force for social cohesion.

My plan for next year is to do some tough talking to these arty types who think the world owes them a living just because they say they're artists. It's about time they realised it's us who'll decide if they're artists not them. With that in mind I'm preparing a list of put-downs I can use to people who patronise me and think I know nowt. While cutting ribbons and flashing smiles for the cameras I'm going to give them what for behind the scenes.

13

My reason for standing down

If you haven't heard by now Tony it must be true what they say — you really are cut off from the world of real people like me. As you ought to have read in the papers, because I leaked it to them, I've decided to resign my seat at the next election. I will miss my constituents, which I'm told are somewhere near Birmingham, and if I had a family I'd probably like to be spending more time with it. The truth is I'm not getting any younger and my knees and back are playing up. I ought to be able to sue this bloody department for injuries incurd during all those nights I've had to spend unconscious in crippling seats while orchestras tootle on and on and actors stand about bawling insults at one another and prancing around with nowt on. And three quid for a small tub of ice cream! And nearly five nicker for a glass of Julio Iglesias! Once bitten twice shy on that score — these days if I know I'm on for the late shift I buy a bag of All Sorts and a Fanta in the local Paki and sit in the lav at half time. They say you can't have too much of the arts but by god Tony I've had the arts up to my flaming earoles. Some weeks I'd do anything for a normal night in watching You've Been Framed. All I can say is thank Christ I'll never have to sit through another second of modern dance or foreign films that go nowhere very slowly and which I can't make head nor sense of.

All my best friends from years back in the Cheshire Cheese keep asking me why I associate with such a bunch of lying sleazebags and part of the truth is, yes, I'm disillusioned too. And completely confused by all the claims the party makes to have sorted everything out when quite obviously we haven't. Yes, Tony, and that means confused with you too. We've not done what we set out to do. And you've never once replied to any of my letters. And you obviously never read that book on art by Jilly Cooper I sent you. You've never once complimented me on my political nouse or on my command of this demanding brief. Honestly though, you try satisfying all these spongers who think the arts are important when so few people really give a monkeys what they do. It's not been easy you know. Only this week I had to unveil in Liverpool a right Isaw which had cost thousands and was completely pointless but which I had to pretend was an uplifting addition to the landscape and quality of life of the poor devils who lived near it and wondered what the hell it was for. It was only an addition to the career of the Spanish twerp what made it. Why do we have to conceal what we really think about this tripe?

I want to make one thing perfectly clear. Perfectly clear. Although I'm surrendering my seat, I intend to stay on as arts minister until the fat lady sings because I know you need me — I wouldn't want to leave you in the soup. And besides, I can't do without the extra wages. I get fifty grand more as a minister so don't think that because I'm leaving I'm not going to be loyal any more. I am. I can't afford to do a Geoffrey Howe and I haven't sat in smoky rooms talking about korums with sweaty beer-swillers for decades only to give up when the lolly's finally rolling in by the sackload. And Connie needs a stair lift putting in for her hips and you can't do those on an MP's basic. No, you can rely on me to keep lying and toe the line until the next election and then someone else can come in and hopefully tell that four-eyed skinny sod where to stick his daft topper.

I was hoping when I came into this job that I'd be able to get more people like me who are not interested in the arts interested. But I can't. I keep pretending that "access" and "broadened participation" are important but they aren't really Tony. It's just a pretend game we play, and we all know it is. You can't sell art to people who don't want it. I understand that because although I've had my eyes opened to a few lovely things while doing this job I can't really be mithered either. If it's a choice between the British Museum and the Cheshire Cheese, the Cheese wins hands down every time. And if it's between some barmy foreign rumpus at the opera and Midsomer Murders there's no contest.

One of these days someone's really going to have to get to grips with the taxpayers' money that goes on the arts. Nearly all the people who go to concerts or theatre could afford to pay the full monty if they had to. And those who fill the museums on the weekend are the better-off too. My mate Pickles is right. Why should he subsidise the pleasures of the rich? We'll be subsidising grouse shooting and Henley Regatta next. No, one of these days somebody will have to put their foot down and say that the arts can either sink or swim. It won't affect me if they shut down the Royal Exchange Theatre or the Royal Shakespeare

Corporation doesn't grace us with their presence at the Opera House for a 'limited season' every autumn.

Don't worry though, I won't rock the boat. I'll stick to the spin. But it doesn't stop me from being bitter Tony. When I look back at how they've laughed at me for being northern and ignorant I realise what I should have done that very first week — pulled the rug from under the bloody lot of em.

14

My bad experience with Raffles

I tell you what though Tony, that lottery's saved our effin bacon. We get the praise for having reinvigorised the arts landscape when the bulk of the cash has come from the lotto. Nice one eh? The other day I was looking down the list of what's happened in the arts in the ten years since we've had lottery cash swilling in: two billion in England alone! Museums keep moaning about being broke but bloody Nora Tony it's been Christmas every day since those numbered balls started flying. And they've all had a slice of cake, what with new this, new that, new extensions and new stuff to hang in them. If that tight Scottish bastard next door to you had had to pay for this lot it would never have happened. But still they whinge! Their appetite for cash is insatiable. The only reason I was look-ing into all this was because some jessie from one of the job creation schemes has been on the blower because he noticed how we've been siphoning off lottery dosh to settle bills normally paid out of income tax. I didn't admit it of course. My view is what does it matter which pot it comes from. Besides, there's bound to come a time when museums have all had their shiny new wings, drive-in lavatories, loft conversions, patios, damp coursing and double glazing all through. As I see it the problem is that museums keep buying more and more stuff only so they can put it in store. Eventually we'll either have to build even more museums or force them to be choosier. Of course if it were up to me I'd tell them that if they want more money they should first sell off all that stuff we've never seen and are never likely to see because it's not entertaining the likes of Pickles stuck down in the cellar is it? Who'd know it had gone except them? Nobody else would give a toss.

I like to keep my little peepers on things so I popped across to the National Picture Gallery in my lunch-time the other day to see an exhibition which I'd read a write-up about in the evening rag. It's about a painter from a while back called Raffles, the one who painted that picture we bought that isn't by him. The director there's another one who's always angling for more jam. He's just opened a new entrance, which is no better than the old one and which had me shuddering because it reminded me of the Co-op's crematorium in Cheetham Hill. I'll probably end up sliding along the rollers there misself so I don't like being reminded of it. Anyway, the dozy slaphead is going to have to start thinking straight. I was shocked I can tell you. First off the exhibition cost nearly a tenner to get in! It looks very posh and like the real McCoy but nine quid is taking the piss if you ask me when we give them so much to be open for nowt. How many folk fiddling benefits can afford that? Then to add insult to injury I was told that I couldn't go in straightaway because there were too many people in already so I'd have to wait in line for half an hour. "I'm the arts minister and I'm in a rush," I said, pulling rank in my teacher's voice. And the ticket woman said to me "That's what they all say Gertie, now get behind the rope." Nine quid to stand in a queue! They should organise it better so that everyone can get in on the spot. Then what happens? I finally gets in and can't see a bleeding thing because it's more packed than a cup tie at Maine Road. It's ridiculous though Tony. They really ought to encourage fewer people. All the time

I was trying to muscle in there were folk pushing me
aside. All of them were well-dressed too and no one
under forty, and not a black face for miles. Back in
my office I got that streak of piss of a director
straight on the blower. And did I give him what for!
"What's all this caper," I said laying it on the
line. "Nine quid and queues for something you can't
see. And where's the ethnic minorities?" "It's a
great success," he said smarmy as you will. "The
crowds are regrettable but the extra cash will enable
us to stay open seven days a week, which is more than
the money you give us allows us to do." I told the
cheeky bastard in no uncertain terms that the next time
I go I want to see some smiling black faces, steel bands
and limbo dancers livening things up and mountains of
steaming yellow rice and samosas in the canteen. Then
I hung up. I was reporting on this at the weekend to
my old pal Pickles in the Cheese and he told me I'd
got it wrong. "Look Ezzie," he said, "Raffles is fine
but he's not for me and you. You're either interested
in art or you're not. And we're not, right? If folk
want to pay a tenner to queue up and see nowt that's
their poison. Me and you'd rather be up Belle Vue for
the stock cars. So what's your problem?" Well Tony,
it's quite obvious to me what the problem is. Belle
Vue doesn't get 25 million smackers every year from
Gordon!

By the way, just a tiny word. If you're deliberising
over the date of the next election try to keep it
until after the end of May because Connie's dead keen
for us to do Can again next year. We're running low
on shampoo and duty frees and our boots could do with
a good shine up. Of course, don't worry, we'll make
out we're batting all guns blazing for the British film
industry.

My brilliant lying over the cuts

I want to let you into a little secret Tony. Do you remember when Blind Jack wrote in his book that I was "thicker than a docker's butty, 110% ignorant about everything artistic and have probably never even read a book without pictures in"? Well strictly ontrenoo, as we teachers say when we're talking behind someone's back, he was spot-on about the ignorant bit. It's hands up time. I admit it. Before I took on this job I hadn't been to the theatre for years except for the New Year's Eve revue Pickles puts on in the upstairs function room of the Cheese. I can't remember the last time I went to a gallery or museum neither. My spirits always sank at the thought of going in a museum. All that frightening silence and concentration and echoing footsteps... I'd rather give blood. And as for books, well, you know, I might buy one for my holidays but I rarely get past the first bonk. Except for Jilly Cooper of course, whose book on art gave me the best possible grounding for this job. Even holiday books aren't for reading really though are they. They're more of a last resort for if your flight's delayed or there's no Sky in the room. For me art is all about a good serial on the telly like that North and South that's just finished. What a corker of a story that was! And set right in the same area of Manchester as the Cheshire Cheese! It looked so true to life which, I think, is what someone famous once said art should be all about. So in this job I've just been going through the motions doing what since time in the memorial has always been assumed is the right thing to do with art, because everyone's too scared to do anything else. But you've got to admit it's a bit of a cheek for me to be trying to get the arts to be meaningful, accessible and socially engaging to the grass roots when I couldn't care a tinker's misself and neither could the rest of

the Cabinet. Oh well, not long to go now before I
hang up my free tickets.

I've been getting some flack for the last few weeks
because the pansies are all up in arms about how little
money they've got from Gordon. Straightaway after the
announcement him with the threadbare topper was on
the blower complaining how the regions wouldn't be
able to buy any Turner Award art for their collections
or put on any challenging and cutting-edge exhibitions.
Between you and me Tony I bet that wanker's never been
further north than Tottenham Court Road. He doesn't
know jack shit about the regions. I told him they
don't want any of his sort of stuff anyway because
nobody goes to see it and when they do they just
stand there laughing at it. That shut him up good and
proper. I was in no mood to take it from him. I had
to sit next to him for hours while they were presenting
the bloody Turner Award — I was missing North and
South as well and had to have Connie video it.
Honestly though Tony you wouldn't believe the crap
they were throwing away good money on. The winner's
work was like one of those diagrams Peter used to
draw for us when he was explaining how to put one
over on the BBC. "Jeffrey Mellor is right up there
at the most challengingly sharp point of the cutting
edge," said the topper. "We wouldn't mind buying it for
our collection but we're short of money." "Go out and
bloody well earn some then," I told him. I've had a
belly full of him complaining about being broke at
the same time as he's coining it from all the kwangos
he sits on. And the food was muck! I had to have the
driver stop for a takeaway on the way home. I watched
the video of North and South with a chicken tikka and
a can of Lilt. Now that's what I call accessible art.

That plonker with the daft red specs from the Arts
Council was next on. He's been complaining that the
cuts would mean real hardship, such real hardship, oh
ever such real hardship, despite the fact he can make
it up by dipping his hands in the lottery dosh that
we stupidly gave him to dole out. Anyway, I came out
fighting and pulled a right flanker on him and the

topper. I showed how his figures were all up the spout by slyly counting previously announced increases in with the new ones. That had him spluttering on the Today programme. He didn't know where he was up to. They always fall for that double-counting stunt. Gordon showed me how to do it over the Christmas pudding last year. "It really throws them when you double up," he said snorting brandy butter into my Baileys. "It buys you time and when they finally realise, it's too late for them not to seem like a bunch of whinging windbags." He's very creative with numbers is Gordon but my god Tony he eats like a navvy. No wonder you never have him over.

Then who should come on but that pip-squeak from England's Heritage who wears his grandad's brogues and looks too young to be doing a paper round. He complained about "the gross betrayal of our history". I've had my eye on England's Heritage for a while. It's run by a load of toffs for another load of toffs. They dream up these barmy schemes to disguise roads by digging under places like Stonehenge when even I can tell that the weight of Stonehenge would make any tunnel collapse. He reeled off a list of 3,500 stately homes and 286 Georgian swimming baths that'll go down the plughole because we're not stumping up. Let them go then, I said. After all, Tony, how many stately homes do we need?

Christmas didn't come a minute too soon I can tell you!

16

My two openings on the same night

By god Tony I've got them by the short and curlies this time! Those museum nancy boys thought they were dealing with a total blockhead. They didn't realise I knew all along they had piles of stuff underground that we couldn't see and which they keep back for only a few select friends to look at. So I've published an instruction to them with a big fancy title: 'Understanding the Past, the Present and the Future: Museums, Access, Centres of Gravity and the Working Man of all Colours, Creeds and Alternative Abilities (But Especially Black) for the New Millennium and Beyond'. Geoffrey helped me word it spot-on and he knows a thing or two about arse-licking the minorities while at the same time shafting the moaning minnies. I told the museums they had to work out what they were doing in this changing and shrinking global world of ours and precisely where they want to go and whether their staff are well adjusted to the challenging spectacles of inclusionism ahead. We'll have the next election in the bag when the grass roots read about this over their Sugar Puffs.

No sooner was it released than the blower was red hot. Him with the horse's bum on his bonce was first up as usual. Did I stop him short! I told him to get some of his spares off on tour around the country. He told me the Tate already had programmes for circulating works around the regions but funds were short. What funds do you need? I asked. Stick them in the back of your Cortina and get them up to the Whitworth. If you can afford half a million for a mirrored ceiling and a room full of mist, sixty notes for petrol and a Kentucky at Knutsford won't break the kitty. He insisted that so much in their collection was not of exhibitable quality but merely for comparative study purposes by scholars. Sod the scholars, I told him, if it's not showable what use is it to the working voter. Get it sold and use the money to send the rest of your good stuff up the M1. And make bloody well sure I see some results before the next election campaign starts. And by the way, I said, how dare you pester me for more money to buy even more clutter when you can't even show what you've got. That shut him up. I tell you Tony it was knockabout stuff.

Then that clever dick of a streak of piss from the National Picture Gallery came on. As a matter of fact minister, he said, all la-di-fuckin-da as though he was talking to a skivvy, far from having a reserve collection we don't have any works that aren't on display. I gave him what for too. That's not what I've heard you bloody lying slaphead, I yelled. Get it all in a Transit up to the Whitworth. They'll have it on the wall faster than a chippy can hang a door. But the nation's greatest pictures are extremely fragile, he said. Well wrap them up in styrofoam then, I told him. That's what Hotpoint do and when was the last time you saw a dent in a new fridge? Believe you me Tony I was on a roll. These people don't seem to realise that the regional museums have told me they're full of people with an appetite to see some classy gear from the smoke. Of course, I know it's bollocks what they tell me about rising attendances. It has to be. Whenever Connie and I have been in the Whitworth at the weekend there's never anyone there, but it's just as well to keep these nancy boys on their toes. Take it from me Tony, when I'm through we'll have the national collections shown nationally and no messing and not bloody well before time neither.

The other night I had to open two exhibitions one after the other and pretend that each was the only one I was going to. My little legs! And talk about fancy footwork! Geoffrey warned me that we'd have to tread gently. That Saatchi bloke was showing a load of new stuff he's bought cheap which he'll be hoping to flog next month at a tidy profit. I've been told he's a fat chancer who'd be just as happy flogging carpets on Grey Mare Lane market. Same night, him with the topper wanted me to open a retrospectual of a sculptor who welds lumps of metal together, a bit like Pickles's mate's wrought iron animals but not half as attractive. Apparently they hate one another these two but they both need to be kept sweet. We have to suck up to Fatso on the off-chance that when he's got bored with his pictures he'll give some of the ones he can't sell to the National Gallery. The topper, meanwhile, hates Fatso because not only has he got a lovely head of hair and can afford better suits but he's got money blowing from every pocket and gets more publicity. Anyway, I rolls up to

Saatchi's drum and, guess what, the cheeky bastard wasn't there to meet me. It turns out he doesn't go to his own openings: I mean, Tony, talk about a bunch of looneys. And the pictures were horrible, sick, and every one far too big even for a lounge in Chorlton-cum-Hardy. The food was top hole mind, very posh, and I sneaked some spicy chicken on dinky wooden skewers into my bag for Connie to have later watching Big Brother. I couldn't see the point of the welded scrap neither. Him with the topper seemed to think it was very important they weren't shown on a stand, like Abraham Lincoln in Albert Square. He called it a very significant moment in the history of 20th century culture when sculpture started sprawling all over the parquet. You could have fooled me. What's on a ragman's cart's more interesting. I wouldn't have given any of em house room.

Roll on the election! At least then I can get back to real life and normal folk and some matching brass elephants on the mantlepiece.

17

My day out with Pickles

You'll be sad to hear, Tony, that the next report will be what the cobbler threw at his wife. I've been in this job for two years during which — and I mean this with all modesty Tony — I've astonished those who doubted I was up to it. I've showed em alright! When it comes to access, inclusion, community regeneration, cultural empowerment, embedding aspirations, outreach beyond the envelope, social diversity, Beethoven in sign language, jackflaps and larty, blind subtitles, Cosy Fan Tooty with HIV, steakholding, wheelchair ramps, not to mention a dozen black Macbeths — one of them set in Soweto, two lesbian Hamlets, Aida in rap and a quadroplegic Henry V, we've improved everything and got everyone involved right down to the last spluttering vegetable. Even the Brussels Eurospongers have had to admit that more people in Britain enjoy the arts than anywhere else in the EU. Didn't I tell you I'd deliver? So, my successor takes over the reins of a tight ship secure in the knowledge that if we're already well in front of them snooty frogs, he's got every reason for telling the usual beggars to bugger off and tread water until the approach of the next election. Why should we spend more cash when we're already streets ahead of Fritz? As my uncle Eddie the baker used to say "Let them eat cake, preferably mine!".

We're winding down in the department because everything's on suspenders until the election's in the bag, so I'd like to take this opportunity to tell you of a real success story. It's one you might consider using on the ustins. One night in the Cheshire Cheese I promised Pickles that before I quit if he came down to the smoke I'd show him the sights all VIP and that. You know, the savvy Londoner shows the hobnailed working man what he's been coughing up for. Well he made it last Tuesday. I told him to throw a sickie, as they all do, but he insisted on taking a day's holiday. I pulled strings in the office and sent him one of my train tickets — no one'll find out. I'd never seen him shaved and in his best kit before so he was a picture when he came off the pendoleeno at Euston looking like Mr C&A with his lunchbox under his arm and his head glinting like a buffed headlamp. I marched him straight off to the National Victoria to see a new exhibition of pictures by Caravedgio which I'd opened the week before. While I was there cutting the ribbon I blagged a couple of free passes off the slaphead who runs it. He sniffed at first but thought better when he realised I might still give him a good shafting before I cleared my desk.

Listening to Pickles as he picked his way through the crowds was ever so moving, Tony, and made me wish I'd done more for labouring folk like him. I learned more looking with Pickles than I did from all the gallery's suits with their flashy specs and fancy lingo. In the first room there were two pictures of the same thing — Jesus having his tea with the disciples —

which seemed a bit pointless to me as there was nowt
to choose between em. Pickles stood for ages weighing
them up. "I could never understand, Ezz," he whispered,
"why the disciples only spotted it was Jesus when he
broke the bread. It's not as though they can't see
his face is it? You can tell they're working men
though. Look at those hands: tough skin, dirty nails.
And the plain clothes and faces like taters. You meet
the same types in the Railway at lunchtime. Rough as
they come and big gestures showing what they think. But
big believers in their own rightness at the same
time. These lads have come straight from work." They
look a bit coarse to me for a religious picture, I
said. "Aye they're common all right, like you and me.
But do you know what's interesting about these two pictures
Ezz? One's all detail on the outside, the other's all
feeling on the inside. It's as though the painter
suddenly realised he didn't need all this posh grub
and decanters. That one with the roast chicken is how
the BBC would do it in a costume drama and this dark
one is how you'd find it round a back entry in a room
lit through an open door that needed oiling."

We wandered about for ages. He said he was sure
that for all the centuries between them he'd have
more in common with Caravedgio than not. He liked the
small pictures best where there was no background and
the artist had concentrated on the faces and hands.
He said he's used to dealing with ordinary people and
recognised the types. I said that one bloke who was
whipping Jesus looked just like Robbie Flockhart, the
weekend barman at the Cheese. "They always have the
same set about them those scallies who enjoy scrapping,"
Pickles said. "Look at him. He loves it. He's itching
to get stuck in, especially when the other bloke's
tied up and can't fight back."

It just goes to show doesn't it Tony that we were
right all along. Everyone's capable of enjoying nice
things. Where we got it wrong though was in blackmailing
museums to water down stuff that's perfectly understandable
already. Eleetism doesn't mean excluding people it
just means settling for the best. I didn't understand

that when I started this job. Pickles is living proof
that where great art's concerned there's no need to
patronise anyone.

18

My meeting with Michaelangelo

I'm writing to you last thing, Tony, before riding
into the sunset after many magical years on board the
gravy train of public service. My desk is cleared and
all that remains is for me to fill a suitcase with
all the staples, file dividers, cartridge paper,
drawing pins, post-it notes (Connie loves these),
pens, highlighters, elastic bands and empty CDs I've
pogged from the stationery cupboard — I don't know
why I'm bothering with CDs as I haven't got a computer
but it's such a lovely blue cellulite box that I
couldn't resist it and I had to wait until everyone
had gone home to nab it. You wouldn't believe the
stuff in that cupboard — there's even a little gadget
like tweezers for pulling out staples which, between
us, is really good for picking your nose when you've
got one of those crusty clingers that won't budge —
it must cost the civil service a fortune. I'll be
well able to last out my retirement without having to
spend a farthing in Rymans. Call it a perk of public
office eh. I feel as though I deserve it for all the
sacrifices I've had to make in order to socially promote
the arts over the last two years.

Geoffrey arranged a little party for me and I was
very touched because lots of the people I deal with
sent leaving presents — books mainly, worse luck. Him
with the daft topper — I'm going to miss that bloody
topper, it's given me and Connie hours of helpless
mirth — sent me a book of his essays which I can't
understand a word of and is going straight to the
back of the grate when I get home. Why write the kind
of bollocks no bugger can fathom? Beats me Tony! The
nancy boy from the Arts Council sent me a rude note
because I forced him to close down lots of organisations

whose names nobody knew and nobody'll miss. He said he
didn't know how people like me could sleep at night
depriving hardworking regional families of access to
the higher concerns of art. I replied — lying of course
— that I'd commissioned a confidential report on how
to close down the Arts Council and left a recommendation
for my successor to act on it at the earliest. He'll
have to hose his knickers out when he reads that!
Geoffrey bought me a lovely picture book of Lowry's
paintings and said he'd miss me because I was the
only normal person he'd ever met.

My last official function was to open an exhibition
of old ornaments and other clobber at the Victoria
and Alfred, which must have recently moved from
Trafalgar Square so it's near all the other museums.
This makes a lot of sense because then the workers
can see them all together, no sweat, in a morning. I
complimented the director — terribly shy bloke, and
even Geoffrey can't remember his name — on this move
in the right direction and he nodded like a judge and
patted my shoulder. I wandered off afterwards because
I was feeling sad. No more free prawn and salad
cream sandwiches at lunch time for me! My god though
Tony they've got some clutter in that V&A. It looks
like an antique shop in Wilmslow and needs a damn
good doing out, but I did come across this really
champion room, high as a church it was. I felt like
Alice wandering into another world. It was full of
sculptures and had that Michaelangelo's David in it.
It was amazing to think that here I am, the arts minister
in charge of the arts, and I never knew this place
existed or that we owned all these works by
Michaelangelo. My little legs were playing up so I
sat down in front of this gigantic boy. By god Tony
I didn't need topperlugs bending my ear about what a
tremendous work that was or what it was about neither.
That look in his eye! It's fright it is. And those
huge hands, gentle and strong. I'd just taped the
little balls in the back of his hand when Geoffrey
suddenly minced into view and asked me all flustered
where I'd been. I told him to show a bit of humbleness

and just look. He asked me why I liked it and I told
him it was because David was obviously so scared and
uncertain of hisself. Even though he's big his body
still seems small, as though he's just a lad and not
confident that he's good enough for the fight ahead.
And then I confessed to him that I really liked it
because it said a lot about me and how I've always
felt that I was never fit for this job. I'd never
felt as though I, me, a teacher of hooligans from
Whalley Range who doesn't know nothing really,
deserved to be filling this important position. I told
him that, although I don't let on, sometimes I go home
at night and I'm terrified by the responsibility, just
like David seems to be. Geoffrey said he could tell
that I felt that way and he did too sometimes. I suddenly
felt very fond of him.

I'm gutted to have missed Can but I've been trying
to wangle misself an invite anyway. I thought I might
be able to swing it if I said I was doing a few
write-ups for the papers but so far only the
Longsight Reporter have replied. You know Tony, I
might just go for a career in journalism! I've quite
enjoyed writing to you, even though you've never once
replied back.

Well, that's it. But just one more thing. I need
to get this off my chest before I head for the hills
and a long retirement of index-linked leisure. TONY,
YOU'RE THE BIGGEST BULLSHITTER I'VE EVER COME ACROSS.
But mum's the word! That's politics eh.

Estelle

P.S. Tony, As I stuffed the last box of drawing pins
into my case just now, I began to have second
thoughts about quitting full time. Is there any
chance you can fit me up with a peerage so I can come
down to the smoke from time to time and collect some
expences and sit on a few well-paid committees to top
up my pension? You know me! I could be a safe pair
of hands to have around the place!